Disturbing Borders

poems by

Alida Woods

Finishing Line Press
Georgetown, Kentucky

Disturbing Borders

For David, My North Star

Copyright © 2018 by Alida Woods
ISBN 978-1-63534-405-9 First Edition
All rights reserved under International and Pan-American Copyright Conventions. No part of this book may be reproduced in any manner whatsoever without written permission from the publisher, except in the case of brief quotations embodied in critical articles and reviews.

ACKNOWLEDGMENTS

"The Clearing" was first published in The 2017 Spring Amsterdam Quarterly

Thank you to my husband, my family, and my teachers.

Publisher: Leah Maines
Editor: Christen Kincaid
Cover Art: Brigitte Knauf
Author Photo: Richard Brown
Cover Design: Dana Irwin

Printed in the USA on acid-free paper.
Order online: www.finishinglinepress.com
also available on amazon.com

Author inquiries and mail orders:
Finishing Line Press
P. O. Box 1626
Georgetown, Kentucky 40324
U. S. A.

Table of Contents

Crossing 1
The Glove 2
Valley of Fire, Utah 3
Folding Lesson 4
Eighty-seven 6
Peripheral Vision 7
Deadheading Daffodils 9
Reckless 10
Cartography 11
The House of Forgetting 12
Pigeon River Gorge 13
Zabriskie Point 14
In the Drawer 15
Triolet to the Comma 16
The Clearing 17
In Your Mother's House 18
Mr. Zip's 19
Cars and Guns 20
Tea with Rosa 22
Where the Spirit Meets the Bone 23
Dancing in Cassadaga 24
 Edisto 26
The Way Summer Sounds 27
Christmas Eve 28
The Color of Morning 29

Crossing

I am watching my daughter
at the top of the stairs,
child on her back
like an old movie.
I see their laughter,
his arms reaching around her neck,
there is no sound.

That night another film,
another country
a woman
harrows a mud-caked field
a loose muslin sling hugs
her child to her back.

Across the border
another,
hijab flapping in the wind,
carries her child,
thin arms clinging
to sinewy shoulders.

Where is that country and
who can find the way
to a place we call home—
the place from which we arrive or depart
refugees, all of us?

We will arrive carrying each other
across the river,
across some faint line in the sand
or we will not arrive.

The Glove

It was missing when
we returned from our walk
along the greenway Sunday afternoon.
Too bad, you said.
I wore them only once—
New Year's Day
when cold cut through
the down and Smart Wool.

Retracing my steps,
I half expect to see
my glove waving from
a branch or fence rail.
I think of lost things:
earrings, signs
posted on poles—
Missing Dog, people
you don't even know
are missing:
three people downriver
in Missouri
or a boy and his mother
crossing some border
in the rain.

Valley of Fire, Utah

Stone speaks
puzzling out a past
of glacial uplift and survival.

Pleated sandstone
pours over
dry ocean floors

metamorphic,
time brushes
against uncounted days.

Desert marigold springs
from Aztec stone.
Flame mallow and prickly pear

push between rain dimpled rock.
Petroglyphs pecked in desert varnish:
atlatl, big horn sheep, rivers

long drained by thermal nudging.
A thick desert wind
carries the mystery forward.

Folding Lesson

In the bow of the boat,
I am eleven.
We are sailing upriver,
away from the harbor mouth.
The island where we will land is a large rock.
Wampanoag called it *Masquesatch*.
The marshes smell of late summer,
water sparks against the side of the boat.

My mother hands me a large wicker basket.
Spoons clatter against
ceramic bowls inside.
My father tethers the boat
and we haul gear up the rock.

Tomorrow we will
drive back to New Jersey
and resume our lives
shored up by summer's end—
suitcases placed on the tail gate then
stacked between dogs and children.

~

Today I prepare for a different journey,
a visit to my mother
in a home that is not her home,
placing shirts, tri-folded in the suitcase.
I have never thought to fold them
otherwise. I watched her
pack a thousand times.

She was the queen of preparedness.
Every detail square:
each sock reunited with its mate
rolled perfectly in our drawers,
percale sheets drawn tightly in hospital corners.
I place the last shirt in the suitcase.

~

I board the plane
placing my bag overhead.
I am sixty-four and I realize
I have forgotten my socks.
They are still balled neatly
in my drawer.

Eighty-seven

She is bent
over pinching up the last
crumbs of chocolate cake
from her plate.
She spins slowly in her scooter,
light catches the halo
of hair upended by static.

From her apartment
in this village of the elderly
day disappears into
the lines on her face.
The woods beyond are
laced with crusted snow, icy
branches scratch the window.

So many lives folded
in the birthday cards
placed upright on the sill. Outside
two finches vie with chickadees
for the last seeds in the feeder.

She is grateful, she says,
for the small birds
which she cannot see. She will listen
tomorrow to the bird call CD
my sister has given her
and to the books on tape,
waiting for the mail, a call from a friend.

Days hang in the balance
between dread and remembrance.
Outside the moon hangs
tiny and fragile in the winter air.

Peripheral Vision

When you called to tell me you could no longer drive
that you were going blind

I was driving down the mountain
into copper colored forests

lapping against
the throat of the French Broad.

Shadows evergreen, cinnamon, persimmon
rippled across the windshield.

~

I am on my way to visit my daughter,
your grand-daughter.

She is studying speech pathology.
My heart catches in my throat.

How could we have known
that not only your eyes

but limbs and words would fail you
leaving you to dark disability?

~

I continue down
to the bottom of the mountain

where loblolly obscure
the ridgeline.

The land flattens out at
foot of the mountains.

It is darker here and deep green.
Clouds hang threatening rain.

I cannot see.

Deadheading Daffodils

A pile of limp yellow blossoms
strewn across the uneven April lawn—
New England is a landscape
softened only slightly
by early spring.
Stone walls spill
over unkempt fields.
Yellow lightens
the slate horizon, urging
brown to green.

My mother planted daffodils
one by one,
hundreds now,
scattered,
yellow along the roadside.

She created this geography:
careful boundaries drawn,
plots of obedient perennials
resurrecting each year
testaments in yellow—
unyielding, resolute.

This is my home—
a landscape austere, immaculate
bursting from the grave of winter.
Yellow catches my breath.

Reckless

Red tulips lap the edges
petals flayed like tongues
necks bending
slim, green.
You say you love them
when they become reckless.

Were you reckless?
Did you want to be?
Your body a stem
lithe in youth,
now bent,
struck by stroke.

The cigarettes, martinis before dinner
always within acceptable measure.
It's what you did.
It's what was done.
You the perfect hostess, everyone agreed.
No one lost control.

And now, your skin
creased by nicotine,
your caviar palette sated
by sweet potato.
The party over.
The tulips droop.

Cartography

I wake in strange waterways
buildings of glass
where I see
everything
and nothing.

I am with you on a ship,
going north.
The cold settles in over the deck.
Our breath against the ocean air
condenses to silence.

Where do we go night after night
on this pilotless craft
heading beyond maps—
a cartographer's dream of empty lines
leading us home?

The House of Forgetting

Photographs stare folded
into a breathless crawl space

stashed under silver tarnished
by neglect.

Spineless cookbooks lean
on dusty shelves into

medical manuals
outdated, unread.

Unasked questions,
dangled like broken bones,

rub against me as I enter
the house of forgetting,

into the room of
ambiguity and contradiction.

December winds take my breath away.
The kitchen door slams behind me.

Pigeon River Gorge

Driving east on I-40
the mountains close in around me.
I am enwombed.
The road narrows
as the landscape pulls me forward
like some suction
drawing me in.
The thin black line points the way.

Two hundred years ago
clouds of passenger pigeons
descended darkening the sky, flooding
farms and orchards.
They flocked in thousands
along the banks of the river
resting on limbs,
weary from migration.

The massacre was easy—
trees removed, hunters for hire.
The meat was cheap and sweet,
squabs shipped by rail, a delicacy.

Martha, the last known pigeon,
died in the Cincinnati Zoo in 1914.
Her resurrected remains
rest in the Smithsonian.
Outside the zoo, a memorial statue.
An entire species extinguished.

The road follows the river
that laps the edges
of thickets crimson and copper
winding through dark history.
The pavement pours forward
into light at the mouth of the gorge,
I am coming home.

Zabriskie Point

The moon pours itself into the folds
of this ancient lakebed.
Under my tongue, a prayer hesitates,
silenced by space.

Undulations of sediment shimmer
into stars scattered on the horizon.
Apparitions of Shoshone and Paiute
rise, constellations above the rim-rock.

Silence fills my eyes.
The prayer, unleashed, hovers
over the badlands, spills
like sorrow at the bottom of time.

In the Drawer

Loose paper clips
strewn beneath coupons
I will forget—
Bed Bath and Beyond 20%,
a restaurant long since out of business.
Thin white phone cords choke
the pencils that have
reproduced in the drawer,
Chap Stick and three tubes of sunscreen.

I find the letter she wrote
two days before she died.
She is chipper and wants to know
how I am. She does not mention cancer
but comments on Monet's Water Lilies
on the face of the card
and the advent of summer.

For some reason I have kept
my sister's letter
under this ungodly mess.
Buried there, it surfaces
when I most need the reminder
that life is messy and unsharpened
pencils, unsent warranties will out-live us.

I close the drawer and get on with the day
forgetting the AAA batteries I was looking for.

Triolet to the Comma

Its' a humble little thing, this mark
Asking you to decelerate, to pause.
Words tumbling on the page just now in park.
It's a humble little thing, this mark.
And on the other side you continue, start
Again to finish the idea, complete the clause.
It's a humble little thing, this mark
Telling you to decelerate, to pause.

The Clearing

The window trembles in leaf light,
shadows lengthen into my daydream.
A chainsaw distances itself
as if to nudge me to consciousness.
Wind rinses leaves, shivering
past the window and I bend
to pat the dog who waits patiently
for a walk.

Her fur ripples in the brittle air
that draws us into this amber afternoon.
Losing light quickly now,
the day falters.

She pulls me into the emerging dusk,
impatient for progress,
determined, and threads our way
back home.

Cutting back through the half-naked wood,
we find a clearing that opens into
a meadow, spongy with mast—
the darkening tree-line.
The moon lifts her belly up
over the trees,
shadows reappear and
ghosts speak softly
of darker woods
windowless and thick.

In Your Mother's House

There were
boxes of boxes
bags of bags and
drawers of drawers
spilling out her life
left on postcards
quilt squares
not sewn together
like the lives
she had not yet lived.
Sweaters to be knit
letters only imagined
days spent in the
taxonomy of things:
sorted packaged
each tidy label
a covenant.
In your mother's house
there was an abundance
of things
a scarcity of love
found in the empty pages
piles of journals
unsent cards
pencils unsharpened.

In the end
when we sorted
through the boxes
her shadow
slid onto
the pages of her
unwritten book.

Mr. Zip's

I turn up the radio and sink
deep into the seat
for the blessed release
of swish and twirl.

The giant blue tentacles
slosh limply over the windshield.
Two sturdy brushes pirouette
along the side of my car.

The final gush of clean
eddies droplets over the
sparkling hood.
I emerge from the sudsy underworld.

My clean car enters the highway.
Banks of salty grey snow
loom before me.
I do not look back.

Cars and Guns

At the light on the corner of
Haywood Street and Montford Avenue

rap music boils inside the adjacent car
like the heart inside my chest

wanting to escape
the red light that holds us both

and keeps us from colliding
with the oncoming Chevy Nova

and the woman with groceries
crossing the street.

The red car pulsing Iggy Azalea
trembles on its high flung haunches.

The driver holds the wheel,
arms extended,

pushes the red light,
almost clipping the curb.

I rumble into the intersection
in my CRV.

49 Killed in Worst Domestic Assault in US
NPR reports.

Hot and impatient
at another red light

I am already late.
For what?

I turn up the radio
feel the thrum of

anger rising in my chest
crushed into an accelerator

as if speed redeemed
or volume absolved our shame.

I pull onto 240
hugging the off-ramp,

sucked into the vortex of cars—
a billboard for Alan's Pawn and Gun.

Tea with Rosa

In the café-bookstore a display
of books for children catches my eye:
*Follow the Drinking Gourd, The Jazz Man,
Martin's Big Words…*
I turn the colorful pages considering
whether my grandson, at two, is too young
for books with "real" pages.

On the cover of a thin paperback
Rosa Parks sits, alone on a bus,
too tidy to have driven the streets of
Montgomery in 1955. The picture,
a caricature, begs the question of the title
Who Was Rosa Parks?

I pick my tea—so many to choose from:
beyond Lady and Earl Grey today I can have
Butcher's Broom—I wonder if it tastes of
dust or straw—or Green Snail Spring,
Silver Monkey, or Nice Red Plum.
There is Gossip Tea and Whistle Sip,
my favorite, Simple Moment Tea.

Rosa sits quietly on the cover of the book
peering over her wire-rim glasses.

Ms. Parks, I ask, if your life had been
made of simple moments and you could
have tea with me, what blend
would you choose?
Hard Times Tea, Back of the Bus,
or maybe just Resist?

Where the Spirit Meets the Bone

The day begins with smallness:
morning coffee, salutations;

the paper dropped in the drive
draws us into the day.

We fold the paper, put away the cup,
tuck our lives into pockets.

Small gestures send us assured
of goodness into the world.

For a moment
we are hostage to hope.

We cannot know the stranger
who offers up the smile

or walks in the shadow of his bones.
We do not know the quiet fear

that drives him into the day, what
has called him to meet his god.

We drop the token into the slot
and take a chance

the train will arrive
at the appointed destination.

Dancing in Cassadaga
> *"Baby, fools pay the price of a whisper*
> *In the night in Cassadaga"* Tom Petty

In the lobby a stuffed bear
rises up on her back legs
warning intruders
that crossing the line may
involve intricate encounters with poetry.

My medium, Torre, who has a
weekly radio show, Venus-in-Velvet,
tells me the bear will ward off
interlopers.

She stops, mid-sentence, raising her
purple-painted nails:
The bear is your totem animal, your protector.

The smell of patchouli permeates
the made-in-India drapery.
Torre draws a small brown bottle of oil from a basket
on the table, holds it at eye level—
Oh Lakshmi, you are strong and elegant.
The smell of burnt leather
contradicts my comfort in her report.

When I ask about my children
she tells me my son is caught
between two worlds and that
he must decide what he wants
to put "out there."
She assures me these two worlds
can co-exist, but repeats,
He must decide.

And that my daughter has seen this life
a time or two.
She is, according to Torre,
a natural mother, also a healer.
I did not reveal that
she just bore my first grandchild
or that she believes in reincarnation.

White suits you, she tells me as she inspects my jacket.
The color of healers.
You were once in Egypt, yes, a ruler of some sort,
a teacher, a wise one. Her eyes roll upward.
It is your voice behind the power of male leaders.
I do not disagree.

I clutch to be sure my jacket is fully zipped,
not wanting to disclose the Emily Dickinson tee I am wearing.
You must write it down. You are guided by a divine voice.
Open yourself to your gifts, listen to your seers.
Her incantation is mesmerizing, inviting.
Did someone tell her I was here with
ten other poets?

A hollow ding sounds.
The stick of incense lies in ashes on the table.
Her fat, breathy voice admonishes me
to stay in the Light and listen well.

Out on the street in downtown Cassadaga,
Sheila, whose last name I do not know,
and I listen to Tom Petty and the Heartbreakers,
Oh baby, now I think I'm starting to believe
the things I've heard
cause tonight in Cassadaga
I hang on every word.

Edisto

Fronds of palm
etch an oyster sky
blushed by the sun setting
over St. Helena Sound.

I walk the empty beach, abundant
with shards of mussel, cracked cockle and jingle
shells covered in barnacles washed up
or dropped by unwary gulls.

At low tide the beach stretches
around Pelican Point—
a conjunction of sound and sea.
The dog's insistent tug pulls me forward.

I round the point where
dunes have been salvaged from an
October hurricane. The water
carries the half moon rising on its back.

Darkness closes.
Only the sound of late pelicans as they
oar their way across the water.
I hear night fall the way rocks listen to the sea.

The Way Summer Sounds

Cardinals call to each other
across the cove
Cha-reep, cha-reep.

Day lilies open, yawning orange,
the brushstroke of a cloud ripples
across silken blueness.

A mower rattles over the
voices of friends on the porch.
This quiet heat falls over me,

slow, sodden
stretching into shadows.
At the end of the lawn fireflies flirt

with disappearing daylight.
The wood thrush's
throaty call thickens

the oncoming dark.
Venus rises
into the voiceless night.

Christmas Eve

Light edges into morning.
A chickadee rests on the sill
her shrill *chick-a-dee-dee-dee*
breaks the silence:
anticipation held in whispers
we exchange
the weight of longing.

The smell of coffee
percolates, pine in the air.
The day unfurls into the corners
of our expectation like ribbons
on gifts strewn under the tree
and the dazzle of lights.

We wait until darkness comes again—
the promise of a child—
so much to ask.

The Color of Morning

I find you in the hall at 4 a.m.
You hear the clucking and coos
and rise osmotic
in the darkness.
You look so young
in spite of your fatigue,
incandescent in love
that knows no contradiction.

Dawn moves in
pulls back the night like
the bedclothes you have shed.
There is a rudeness in the
apparitions that appear
one by one
against the color of morning:
a car in the street, the mailbox,
the tree-line over the fence.
Borders disturb the intimacy of blackness.

But here you are
in the hall, child in your arms,
no edges or boundaries.

A native of New England, **Alida Woods** now lives in the mountains of Western North Carolina, where she has escaped the winters of the Northeast. Her family home on the south coast of Massachusetts deeply informs her work as do nuanced landscapes of the south and the lives of ordinary people in everyday places. Her writing life was strongly influenced by Nancy Willard at Vassar and the shadows cast by Edna St. Vincent Millay and Elizabeth Bishop while at Vassar.

Her life has been spent largely among school children as a teacher, school principal, and a mentor. She continues to work on behalf of children in her work in social justice and non-profits in Asheville, North Carolina.

Here she enjoys her home in the historic Montford neighborhood which she shares with her husband, David, their dog and often with her extended family and friends.

She is indebted to her family for their love and support and for her mentors Eric Nelson, Katherine Soniat, Tina Barr, and to the Great Smokies Writing Program.

Her work has appeared in *The Avocet, The Great Smokies Review, The Westward Quarterly, Front Porch,* and *The Amsterdam Quarterly.*

www.ingramcontent.com/pod-product-compliance
Lightning Source LLC
LaVergne TN
LVHW041511070426
835507LV00012B/1490